Thunderstorm

Catherine Chambers

Heinemann Library
Chicago, Illinois

© 2002 Reed Educational & Professional Publishing
Published by Heinemann Library,
an imprint of Reed Educational & Professional Publishing,
Chicago, Illinois

Customer Service 888-454-2279

Visit our website at www.heinemannlibrary.com

Designed by Visual Image
Illustrations by Paul Bale
Originated by Ambassador Litho
Printed and bound in South China

06 05 04 03 02
10 9 8 7 6 5 4 3 2 1

Library of Congress Cataloging-in-Publication Data
Chambers, Catherine, 1954-
  Thunderstorm / Catherine Chambers.
    p. cm. -- (Wild weather)
Summary: Describes how thunderstorms are formed; the lightning, thunder,
winds, and rains that are part of them; and the impact of these storms
on plants, animals, and humans.
Includes bibliographical references and index.
  ISBN 1-58810-653-5 (HC), 1-4034-0115-2 (Pbk)
  1. Thunderstorms--Juvenile literature. 2.
Thunderstorms--Physiological effect--Juvenile literature. [1.
Thunderstorms.] I. Title. II. Series.
  QC968.2 .C48 2002
  551.55'4--dc21
                                2002000822

Acknowledgments
The author and publishers are grateful to the following for permission to reproduce copyright material: p. 19 Associated Press; pp. 5, 9, 27, 28 Corbis; p. 24 Image Bank; p. 25 Oxford Scientific Films; p. 26 PA Photos; pp. 7, 15, 22 Photodisc; pp. 4, 11, 16, 29 Science Photo Library; p. 20 Stock Market; pp. 6, 10, 12, 14, 17, 18, 21, 23 Stone.

Cover photograph reproduced with permission of Science Photo Library.

The Publishers would like to thank the Met Office for their assistance in the preparation of this book.

Every effort has been made to contact copyright holders of any material reproduced in this book. Any omissions will be rectified in subsequent printings if notice is given to the publisher.

Some words are shown in bold, **like this.** You can find out what they mean by looking in the glossary.

Contents

What Is a Thunderstorm? 4

Where Do Thunderstorms Happen? 6

How Do Thunderclouds Form? 8

Why Do Thunderstorms Happen? 10

What Are Lightning and Thunder? 12

What Are Thunderstorms Like? 14

Rain and Hail 16

Harmful Lightning 18

Preparing for Thunderstorms 20

Coping with Thunderstorms 22

Nature and Thunderstorms 24

To the Rescue! 26

Adapting to Thunderstorms 28

Fact File 30

Glossary 31

More Books to Read 32

Index 32

What Is a Thunderstorm?

A thunderstorm is a powerful storm with strong winds and heavy rain. Thunderstorms are different from regular storms because they include thunder and lightning.

The rain from thunderstorms can cause **floods.**
Hail can break windows and ruin **crops.**
Lightning can strike trees and houses. Strong
winds can blow down trees and power lines.

Where Do Thunderstorms Happen?

Thunderstorms happen in many parts of the world. They happen most often in places where the sun is very hot and the air is very moist. Many of these areas lie in or near the **Tropics.**

This island lies in the Tropics. A lot of thunderstorms happen here. When the storms roll in from the sea they can bring a lot of rain and strong winds.

How Do Thunderclouds Form?

Thunderclouds usually form when there is a lot of **water vapor** in the air. The vapor makes the air feel **humid.** When the vapor rises and cools, huge storm clouds form.

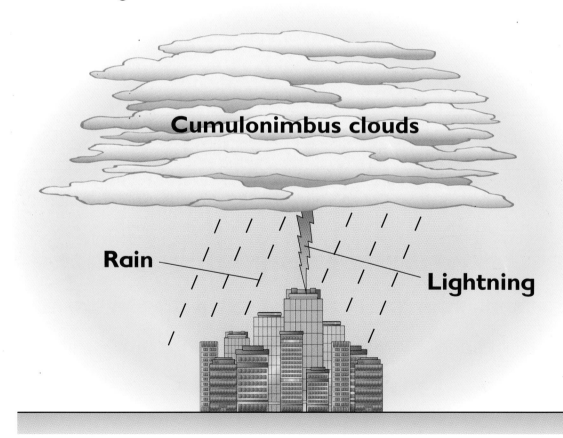

Cumulonimbus clouds

Rain

Lightning

The clouds that cause thunderstorms are called cumulonimbus clouds. They look like big piles of fluffy clouds. Cumulonimbus clouds are very tall, but their bottoms can lie close to the ground.

Why Do Thunderstorms Happen?

When the tiny drops of water inside a thundercloud join together, they become heavier. When they get to be heavy enough, they fall to the ground as drops of rain.

Electricity builds up inside the clouds. This electricity is then released in a bright flash of lightning. The lightning causes thunder to rumble through the air.

What Are Lightning and Thunder?

Lightning is the bright flash you see when **electricity** is released from a cloud. There are different types of lightning. This picture shows forked lightning traveling from the clouds to the ground.

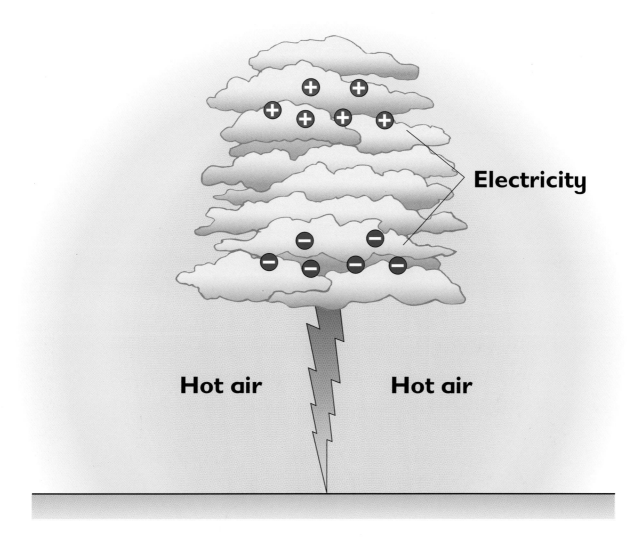

Electricity

Hot air   Hot air

Thunder is the loud crash you hear when lightning is released. Lightning heats up the air very quickly. The air **expands** with a loud crack.

What Are Thunderstorms Like?

The sky goes very dark before a thunderstorm. Then the wind becomes stronger. Heavy rain starts to pour down. Sometimes frozen drops of water fall. These are called **hailstones.**

Lightning flashes across the sky. It is followed by thunder. We always see the lightning before we hear the thunder. This is because light travels to us more quickly than sound.

Rain and Hail

A lot of rain can fall during a thunderstorm. This can cause **flash floods** in rivers or on roads. The water can break bridges or trap people in their homes and cars.

Thunderstorms can also bring balls of ice called **hailstones.** Some hailstones are as big as tennis balls. They can hurt people and animals. Hailstones can also damage **crops.**

Harmful Lightning

The island of Saint Lucia is in the Caribbean Sea. Sometimes heavy thunderstorms happen here. The storms can cause a lot of damage.

If lightning strikes trees and buildings it can set them on fire. It can cause forest fires when it strikes trees. If lightning strikes people or animals it can **injure** or kill them.

Preparing for Thunderstorms

Weather experts collect information about the weather so that they can predict what will happen. If a thunderstorm is coming, warnings will usually be carried on television and radio stations. Then people can prepare for the storm.

Thunderstorms can bring strong winds. They can also bring lots of heavy rain. Some farmers move their animals to high ground to keep them safe from **floods.**

Coping with Thunderstorms

Don't stay outside during a thunderstorm! The rain will get you very wet. The storm can also knock down trees and power lines. Lightning can strike people, but it does not happen very often.

Trees standing alone are often struck by lightning. Don't try to take **shelter** under trees during a thunderstorm.

Nature and Thunderstorms

Animals are often frightened by thunder. They can also get struck by lightning in open fields. Some farmers move their animals inside during a thunderstorm.

Lightning can strike tree trunks and burn them. Many trees have a kind of sticky sap underneath the **bark.** This oozes out and seals up the burned trunk.

To the Rescue!

The heavy rain from thunderstorms can cause **flash floods.** Water in rivers and sewers rises quickly and floods the roads nearby. People in cars can get trapped by these floods. Sometimes helicopters rescue people from the water.

Lightning can set fire to dry trees and plants.
This can lead to big forest fires. Firefighters try
to put the fires out. They rescue people who are
trapped by the flames.

Adapting to Thunderstorms

Some buildings have metal **lightning rods** to protect them from lightning. A metal wire runs from the rod down the side of the building. It takes the **electricity** away from the building and into the ground, where it will not do any damage.

This is the Eiffel Tower in Paris, France. Tall buildings like this are more likely to be struck by lightning. Lightning rods keep people from being hurt by the lightning.

Fact File

◆ A flash of lightning is usually made up of many different flashes. They happen so fast that they look like a single flash.

◆ Lightning heats the air around it. It can make air hotter than the surface of the Sun. As the air heats up it makes the sound we call thunder.

◆ Forked lightning streaks towards the ground. Sheet lightning seems to flash from behind a cloud. But they are really the same kind of lightning. They look different depending on how far away you are.

Glossary

bark hard covering of a tree or bush's trunk and main stems

crop plants grown for food

electricity form of energy that provides power to run machines

expand to get bigger

flash flood sudden flood caused by heavy rain

flood overflow of water onto a place that is usually dry

hail small balls of ice that sometimes fall from thunderclouds

hailstone single piece of hail

humid containing a lot of moisture

injure to hurt someone

lightning rod metal rod that conducts the electricity from a lightning strike down to the ground

shelter safe place

Tropics very warm parts of the world on either side of the Equator

water vapor water that has changed into a gas

More Books to Read

Ashwell, Miranda, and Andy Owen. *Rain.* Chicago: Heinemann Library, 1999.

Branley, Franklyn M. *Flash, Crash, Rumble, & Roll.* New York: HarperCollins Children's Book Group, 1999.

Saunders-Smith, Gail. *Lightning.* Danbury, Conn.: Children's Press, 1998.

Index

animals 17, 21, 24
clouds 8, 9, 10, 12
crops 5, 17
cumulonimbus clouds 9
damage 5, 16, 17, 18, 19, 20
electricity 11, 12, 28
farming 21, 24
floods 5, 16, 21, 26
forest fires 19, 27
hailstones 5, 14, 17
humidity 8
lightning 4, 5, 11, 12, 13, 15, 19, 22, 23, 24, 25, 27, 28, 29, 30
lightning rods 28, 29
rain 4, 5, 7, 10, 14, 16, 21, 22
thunder 4, 11, 13, 15, 24, 30
trees 5, 19, 22, 23, 25, 27
Tropics 6, 7
water vapor 8
winds 4, 5, 7, 14, 21

Nature's Children

EELS

John Woodward

GROLIER

FACTS IN BRIEF

Classification of Eels

Class: *Osteichthyes* (bony fishes)

Order: *Anguilliformes* (eels); *Gymnotiformes* (electric eel)

Family: There are 15 families of eels, including one family of freshwater eels *(Anguillidae)*. The electric eel is the only member of the *Electrophoridae* family.

Genera: There are 141 genera of eels.

Species: There are at least 738 species of eels.

World distribution.   Worldwide in all oceans. Also in fresh waters, especially in North America, Europe, south Asia, and Australia.

Habitat.   Rivers, lakes, ponds, estuaries, shallow seas, deep oceans.

Distinctive physical characteristics.   Long, thin body like a snake, with no obvious scales. Ribbonlike fins top and bottom, and a pair of small "pectoral" fins at the front.

Habits.   Freshwater eels live mainly near the bottom and hunt for food by night. Most marine eels live in rocky crevices.

Diet.   Mainly small fish and other water creatures.

© 2004 The Brown Reference Group plc
Printed and bound in U.S.A.
Edited by John Farndon and Angela Koo

Published by:

**An imprint of Scholastic
Library Publishing
Old Sherman Turnpike, Danbury,
Connecticut 06816**

Library of Congress Cataloging-in-Publication Data

Woodward, John, 1954–
    Eels / John Woodward.
      p. cm. — (Nature's children)
    Includes index.
    Summary: Describes the physical characteristics, habits, and behavior of eels.
    ISBN 0–7172–5957–9 (set)   ISBN 0–7172–5962–5
    1. Eels—Juvenile literature. [1. Eels.] I. Title. II. Series.

QL637.9.A5W66 2004
597'.43—dc21

                                      2003049166

Contents

What Is an Eel?   Page 6

Eel Variety   Page 9

Shape and Size   Page 10

Inside an Eel   Page 13

Where Do Eels Live?   Page 14

Getting Around   Page 17

Freshwater Eels   Page 18

Conger Eels   Page 21

Moray Eels   Page 22

Garden Eels   Page 25

Deep Sea Eels   Page 26

Eel Lookalikes   Page 29

Electric Eel   Page 30

Eel Enemies   Page 32

Into the Blue   Page 33

Midocean Mystery   Page 36

Leafy Larvae   Page 39

Long Drift   Page 40

Heading for Home   Page 43

Eels and People   Page 44

Eels in Danger   Page 46

Words to Know   Page 47

Index   Page 48

Eels are long, slender fish that look a little like snakes. They are easy to recognize, although not all long, snaky fish are true eels. The eels many people know are freshwater eels that swim far up rivers. But many other eels live in the remote ocean, including some real monsters of the deep.

Eels have a strange, snakelike shape. Eels that live in the deep oceans have even stranger features. But the really amazing thing about eels is their life history. You may have eels living in a river near you, but they do not live there all the time. They may have traveled thousands of miles to get there, crossing huge oceans on the way. Their parents may have traveled thousands of miles, too, changing their shape, color, and almost everything else about their bodies in the process. No one really knows why eels do this.

As night approaches in the western Atlantic ocean, a green moray eel emerges to hunt fishes and crabs.

What Is an Eel?

Opposite page:
These big tropical fish are called tarpons. They look like most other fish. But they began life as almost see-through leaflike creatures, just as eels do.

An eel looks a little like a snake, but it is really a kind of bony fish. Like other fish, it has gills for absorbing vital oxygen from the water. Like most other fish, too, it has a bony skeleton. Sharks and rays are different: Their skeletons are made of flexible cartilage.

There are two things about an eel that make it quite different from a typical bony fish like a salmon or a cod. The first is its snaky shape. All eels are this shape, and the shape has an important effect on the way they live. The second is that an eel starts life looking very different from its parents. Other baby fish look like small fish, but a baby eel is more like a transparent leaf with a tiny head at one end. Only three other types of fish apart from eels have these leafy babies, or larvae. These other types are big, silvery tarpons, similar bonefish, and odd, rather eel-like notacanths.

Spotted snake eels like this burrow in the sand of the seabed in the Indian and west Pacific oceans.

Eel Variety

At the last count there were 738 species (types) of eels. There may be more still to be discovered. Most of these eels live in the oceans. They include the conger eels and the moray eels, which lurk among rocks and wrecks in shallow seas. There are also many strange-looking eels with names like snake eels, cut-throat eels, worm eels, and duckbill eels. Weirdest of all are the snipe eels and gulper eels, which live in the dark depths of the deep oceans.

The 16 eel species that live in rivers and lakes all belong to one family of closely related eels: the freshwater eels, or Anguillidae (said ang-GWEE-li-die). They include the American eel, European eel, and Japanese eel. All three types look very alike and live in the same way. Although they spend most of their lives in fresh water, they all migrate back to the ocean to breed.

Shape and Size

All eels are long and bendy. Some are so elongated that they are called spaghetti eels. Many have extremely long, slender tails. The tails are so fragile that they can break off when the eels are caught.

Unlike other fish, eels do not have many paired fins on their bodies. A typical eel has just one pair of short fins near its head. It also has an extremely long dorsal fin that extends right down its back to the tip of its tail. It also has a similar fin at the back that extends along the underside of its tail. It has no true tail fin.

The biggest eels can grow up to 10 feet (3 meters) long or even more. Female freshwater eels normally grow to about 40 inches (1 meter), but males are only half as long. Really big freshwater eels can often weigh 28 pounds (13 kilograms), but 10 pounds (4.5 kilograms) is more usual.

Inside an Eel

A typical eel's body is mostly muscle, with a small cavity for its stomach and other vital organs. The muscle is attached to a very long backbone. Many other animals have backbones, including humans. What makes an eel's backbone special is its length and bendiness. Backbones are made up of many small bones called vertebrae, which act like hinges. Our backbones have just 33 vertebrae. One type of snipe eel has 750, the biggest number ever found in any animal! All these vertebrae make the eel really bendy.

An eel's head is usually small. Unlike some eel-like fish, it has true jawbones equipped with teeth. Many eels have tubular nostrils that they use to test the water for the scent of prey. Most eels have good eyesight, too.

Behind the eel's head are flaps that cover its gills. The gills are clusters of feathery tubes filled with blood. They absorb oxygen from the water and get rid of waste carbon dioxide in much the same way as our lungs breathe.

Opposite page: Eels have gills for breathing just like other fish. The gill flaps that cover the gills are the shiny silver disks on the side of the head of this common eel.

Where Do Eels Live?

Most of the world's eels live in shallow seas, where the sunlight reaches the seabed. They generally hide in crevices on the seafloor, waiting for prey to come their way. Since sunny, shallow waters teem with marine life, the eels never have to wait long.

Some eels live in the deep oceans, in the gloomy "twilight zone" below the sunlit surface waters. Down there eels can't survive by waiting in crevices because there is so little to eat in the dark, very cold water. So deep-ocean eels swim or drift in the open ocean.

Freshwater eels live for a while in the ocean, but most of their lives are spent in rivers and lakes. They can put up with any sort of water, from clear, rocky rivers to muddy ditches and ponds. They live on the bottom and may spend the winter buried in the mud.

Getting Around

An eel swims by wriggling like a snake. It uses the big muscles attached to its backbone to pull its body into a rippling wave. By making the wave move from head to tail, it pushes itself forward through the water. Most fish use much the same method, but they have big fins to help and can swim a lot faster.

Wriggling is not a very efficient way of swimming, but it has one big advantage: It works on land, too. Freshwater eels can survive out of water for a long time because they carry their own water supply for breathing. If an eel runs out of food, it can slither overland through wet grass to find itself a better place to live.

Most fish waggle their fins to move through the water faster. This zebra moray eel wriggles its entire body.

Freshwater Eels

*You can sometimes
see freshwater eels
on land, slithering
at night through
dew-soaked grass
from one stream
to another.*

Freshwater eels are amazingly tough, successful fish. They can live in almost any kind of water. Their skin is protected by a thick layer of slime that makes them extremely slippery. That helps them avoid injury. The slime also keeps an eel from drying out if it has to make an overland trip to another river or lake. Usually, though, the eel chooses a wet night for the journey.

Freshwater eels eat virtually anything they can catch and swallow. Most of their victims are insects, snails, worms, frogs, newts, and tadpoles, but they also catch small fish and steal fish eggs. Big eels sometimes grab small water birds swimming on the surface. Freshwater eels often hunt at night. They use scent to track down prey and smelly scraps such as the remains of dead animals.

Conger Eels

The conger eels are big, muscular eels that live in rock crevices and inside the rusting hulks of sunken ships in the sea. The common conger of the North Atlantic Ocean and the Mediterranean Sea is built like a python and grows to 9 feet (2.7 meters) long.

A conger usually stays in its lair during the day and emerges at night to hunt for fish, crabs, and octopuses. Its big eyes help it see in the gloom; and like most eels, it has a good sense of smell. A row of pressure sensors along its flanks, called the lateral line, picks up vibrations in the water. The sensors often lead the eel to trapped fish struggling in fishing nets. Once it grabs a victim in its short, sharp teeth, the conger swallows it whole. A conger eel may shake big crabs and lobsters to break off their claws.

Opposite page: *The conger eel is a fearsome hunter with very powerful jaws. At night it lies in ambush on the seabed, then pounces on fish like this unlucky yellow tang.*

Moray Eels

Fierce moray eels live in warm seas all over the world. There are about 200 different species. Some are drab creatures, like the dark brown California moray. Others are vividly patterned with bright colors, like the white-striped zebra moray and the dragon moray that live in reefs in warm, shallow seas. Some of the morays that live on reefs have strange horns and "leaves" on their noses. These leaves may help the morays sniff out prey. Many morays have very long, needle-sharp teeth for seizing slippery fish, and these teeth can give a nasty bite. In ancient Rome the ruler Nero was said to have thrown disobedient servants into pits of hungry moray eels.

A moray stays hidden in its rock or reef crevice by day. It gets more active at night, lunging after passing fish and other animals. But it usually keeps its tail wedged securely in its lair. That way it can make a quick retreat from bigger, fiercer fish like sharks.

This may look like patch of dead sea plants. It's not;
it's a colony of garden eels, poking their heads up.

Garden Eels

Some of the strangest eels are the garden eels. Garden eels live in colonies on the sandy seabeds of warm, shallow seas. At night they rest in burrows that are only a few inches apart. During the day they emerge to feed on food particles swept past by the current. They rear up and bend their heads over to face the flow. Meanwhile, they keep their tails rooted in their burrows, so they look like plants waving around in the breeze.

Garden eels hardly ever leave their burrows in the seabed. They usually retreat very quickly if there is any sign of danger. Male eels try to move in next to females so they can mate with them in the breeding season. If there are no females nearby, a male may move to another burrow to be nearer a female.

Deep Sea Eels

Opposite page: *Down in the dark of the deep ocean it pays to be seen —to attract both prey and a mate. That is why eels that live in the deep, like this one, glow brightly.*

The weirdest of all eels live in the open water of the deep oceans, including some that glow in the dark. Some deepwater eels are called snipe eels. Snipe eels have incredibly long, slender bodies. They also have peculiar jaws like curved needles covered in tiny teeth. The jaws flare apart rather than meeting in the usual way. No one really knows how snipe eels catch their prey. They feed mainly on deep-sea shrimp. Some scientists think that the long legs and antennae of the shrimps get entangled in the snipe eels' jaws.

Gulper eels are even more peculiar. They have whiplike tails, huge mouths, and elastic stomachs like balloons. Food is very scarce in the deep, dark oceans, so gulper eels are equipped to catch and eat anything they find. One type even has a tip to its tail that glows in the dark. This glowing tip may lure victims within range of its vast mouth.

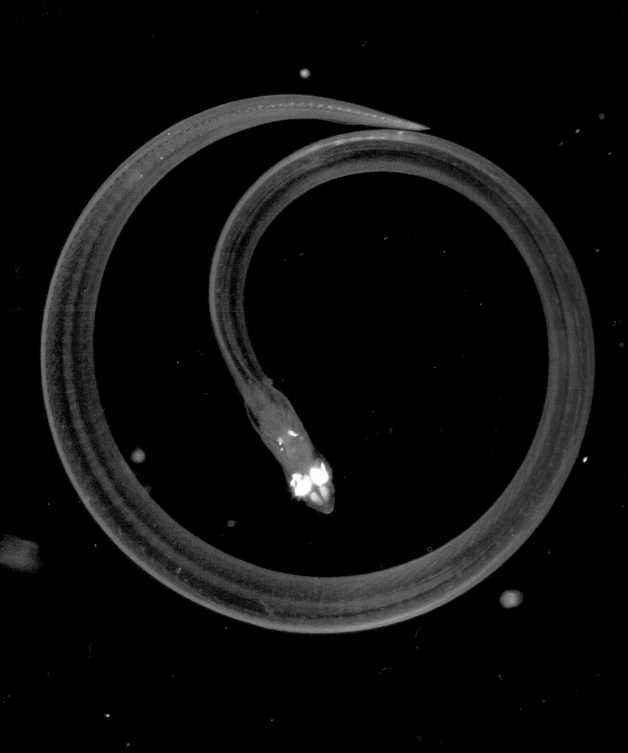

Eel Lookalikes

Eels are not the only snakelike fish. There are plenty of others, including some strange creatures called lampreys and hagfishes. Neither lampreys nor hagfish have bony skeletons. Nor do they have true jaws or teeth. A lamprey's mouth is ringed with razor-sharp serrations, like little teeth. A lamprey feeds by latching onto other fish with these notches and sucking its victim's blood. Some lampreys feed on other living fish by rasping holes in their sides and sucking their juices. The hagfish is even odder. It is horribly slimy and has no eyes. It feeds by boring into the bodies of dead fish that fall to the seabed.

Other eel lookalikes include sand eels. They are small, slender, silvery fish that live mainly in the North Atlantic. You can tell they are not true eels because they have real tail fins. Puffins eat a lot of sand eels. The puffins catch them underwater, then carry them back to their nest burrows in their big multicolored beaks. Trawlers catch sand eels for cat food.

Opposite page:
A puffin carries its latest catch of sand eels back to its burrow.

Electric Eel

In the Amazon River of South America lives a kind of eel called an electric eel. Although it is called an eel, it is not related to other eels. In fact, it is a cousin of catfish and carp.

The waters of the Amazon are often very muddy and murky. But an electric eel finds its way—and its prey—by sending out pulses of electricity. The electricity is generated in musclelike organs in the eel's tail. The pulses bounce off things nearby to give the eel a "picture" just as an aircraft's radar does.

The pulses the eel sends out to find its way are quite weak. But an electric eel also has extra electric organs running right down its back. With these extra organs it can send out a powerful surge of electricity of up to 650 volts, which is nearly six times the amount supplied to the wall sockets in your home. That's powerful enough to stun a horse—and it could knock a person stone dead.

Electric eels live in the murky waters of the Amazon River and send out electric pulses to find their way.

Eel Enemies

Eels that live out at sea have many enemies, including other eels such as conger eels. A full-grown conger eel will even eat other congers. Garden eels fall victim to rays. Rays are huge, flat fish with giant winglike fins. They slice through the eel colonies like underwater lawnmowers.

For freshwater eels the dangers are otters and herons. Eels swim so slowly that otters find them easy to catch. An otter snatches an eel in its mouth, then swims quickly to shore. There the otter holds its victim in its claws and tears it apart with its sharp teeth.

Herons may also prey on eels because they are easy targets. Herons probably find a big, slimy eel easy to swallow whole, too. A heron stands in the shallows until an eel passes. Then, lunging forward, the heron grabs the eel with its bill and flips it around to swallow it headfirst. A quick gulp, and it's gone.

Into the Blue

Freshwater eels live and feed happily in rivers for most of their lives. But after 6 to 20 years they get an urge to breed. So off they swim downriver to the sea. As an eel nears the ocean, its body begins to change. Its head gets more pointed, and its eyes grow large. Its back turns darker, and its sides take on a silvery sheen. By the time it reaches the sea, it stops eating altogether. This is surprising because it has a long journey ahead of it.

Many eels just disappear into the ocean. No one knows where they go. American and European eels head for a region of the North Atlantic near Bermuda. It is called the Sargasso Sea and is especially rich in food. European eels swim more than 3,000 miles (4,830 kilometers) to get there. Since eels are slow swimmers, the trip may take seven months or even longer. By the time they arrive, the eels are ready to breed.

Midocean Mystery

Like many fish, eels lay millions of eggs. This is called spawning. The eels that spawn in the Sargasso Sea probably release their eggs deep in the water. Then they die, exhausted by their long journey from their home rivers.

Exactly why they swim so far is a mystery. The Sargasso Sea is an area of quiet water at the center of the great swirl of ocean currents circling the North Atlantic. It is famous for the seaweed that floats at its surface. The Sargasso Sea is warm and calm, and may be ideal for the tiny eel larvae (young) that hatch from the eggs. But their parents have to make a huge effort to reach it, and the baby eels have to make a long journey back again. Scientists think that the eels started making the trip long ago when the Atlantic was smaller, and they never lost the habit.

In the Sargasso Sea weird tangles of floating seaweed called sargassum provide a rich breeding ground for eels.

Leafy Larvae

When they first hatch, baby eels are called larvae. The eel larvae that hatch in the Sargasso Sea are peculiar creatures. They look a bit like the leaves of a willow tree and are almost completely transparent. They are barely 0.4 inches (1 centimeter) long.

Each larva has a tiny head that develops odd, forward-pointing teeth. These teeth don't seem to be very useful for eating. It seems likely that a baby eel doesn't really eat in the way that bigger fish do. Instead, it probably absorbs food particles through the thin lining of its mouth, soaking them up like a sponge. The larvae of other eels such as conger eels certainly do this. For a while after hatching, the common eel larvae drift in the warm, clear water of the Sargasso Sea. There they are at the mercy of the ocean currents as well as any hungry animals that pass by.

Opposite page:
The larvae, or young, of eels hatched in the Sargasso Sea look more like leaves than fish. You can just make out a tiny eye and mouth at one end.

Long Drift

The baby eels spawned in the mid-Atlantic eventually get caught up in ocean currents and carried away from the Sargasso Sea. Some end up in the Caribbean Sea, but most are swept northeast in the powerful current known as the Gulf Stream. It carries baby American eels to the Atlantic coasts of the United States and Canada. The current also takes European eels all the way across the Atlantic to western Europe and the Mediterranean.

The journey can take a year or more. As they drift across the ocean, the leafy larvae grow bigger. This shows they must be eating something. When they reach the coast, they swim into fresh water flowing from rivers. The fresh water makes their bodies change dramatically. First, the larvae start to shrink. Then their long, leafy bodies stretch, and they become almost transparent, like glass—which is why they are often called glass eels.

As these eels swim into a river for the first time, they
grow long and thin. They are almost as clear as glass.

Heading for Home

Some eels stay in the shallow waters of coastal bays and never move into fresh water. But most eventually swim away from the sea into rivers and start to make their way upstream. The transparent glass eels start using their mouths to eat properly. Gradually, the eels turn brown with yellow flanks. But they are still tiny, wormlike creatures, now called elvers.

Elvers swim upstream against the river flow, following their instinct. If the elvers get to rapids and waterfalls, they squirm their way up the quietest sections. Many are probably swept away and even killed. Others manage to reach the calm waters above the rapids and continue their journey. Many elvers swim far inland, right up the Mississippi River network or deep into central Europe. Eventually they stop and settle down to grow into big, powerful freshwater eels like their parents.

Opposite page:
As they enter a river and begin to struggle upstream against the current, glass eels begin to turn into small, brownish elvers

Eels and People

Opposite page:
This ancient Roman mosaic from Tripoli in North Africa shows a moray eel. The Romans kept moray eels as pets.

In the days of the Roman Empire, two thousand years ago, wealthy Romans used to keep moray eels as pets. They must have been very expensive, because only the richest people had them. One Roman called Gaius Herrius had such a magnificent collection of moray eels that the emperor Julius Caesar asked if he could buy them!

More recently, moray eels have earned a bad reputation among divers because many have very long teeth and often bite. The bites can get infected, and some divers believe that a moray's bite is poisonous.

Freshwater eels have been caught and used for food throughout history. They are also raised on special eel farms. The eels are smoked over wood fires like smoked salmon to give them a rich flavor. The heat also cooks them. This is just as well, because raw eel blood contains a very dangerous poison that is only destroyed by cooking.

Eels in Danger

Freshwater eels are still harvested and eaten in huge numbers around the world, especially in countries such as Japan and Taiwan. But they are not so common as they were. No one knows quite why, but it seems likely we humans are to blame.

We may be catching too many eels too young, before they have a chance to breed. Dams built across rivers may also be stopping the eels swimming upriver. There are now over 15,000 dams across streams flowing into the Atlantic, blocking off 84 percent of the eels' natural homes. The streams have been polluted by factories, too. Eels suffer especially from this because they live so long.

But some scientists think the eels' problems could be natural. Some think changes in the world climate have diverted ocean currents. So the eel cannot follow its normal migration routes. Whatever the cause, eels are still common. Let's hope they stay that way.

Words to Know

Antennae The long "feelers" of shrimp, insects, and many other small animals.

Carbon dioxide The waste gas produced by the bodies of all animals as they turn food into energy.

Cartilage The flexible material that supports our ears and noses, which forms the skeletons of sharks.

Colony A group of animals that live together or breed together.

Dorsal fin The fin in the center of a fish's back that extends to the tail of an eel.

Gills Organs that absorb oxygen from water and get rid of waste carbon dioxide.

Instinct Something that an animal knows without being taught.

Lateral line The line of pressure sensors along a fish's flank.

Lure A type of bait that cannot be eaten.

Migrate To make a long journey to find food or to breed.

Larva (plural larvae) A young form of an animal, which is quite different from its parents.

Spawn To produce eggs that are then fertilized by a male.

Species A particular type of animal.

Vertebrae The bones that link together in a chain to form an animal's backbone.

INDEX

backbone, 13, 17
breeding, 9, 25, 33, 46

carbon dioxide, 13
conger eel, 9, 21, 32, 39; *illus.*, 20

deepwater eels, 14, 26; *illus.*, 27
dragon moray, 22; *illus.*, 23

eggs, 36
electric eel, 30; *illus.*, 31
electricity, 30
elvers, 43; *illus.*, 42

fins, 10, 17, 29
freshwater eel, 5, 9, 10, 14, 17, 18,
 32, 33, 43, 44, 46; *illus.*, 19

garden eel, 25, 32; *illus.*, 24
gills, 6; *illus.*, 13
glass eel, 40, 43; *illus.*, 41
gulper eel, 9, 26

hagfish, 29
heron, 32

lampreys, 29
larva, 6, 36, 39, 40; *illus.*, 38

migration, 9, 46
moray eel, 9, 22, 44;
 illus., 11, 15, 17, 23

otter, 32
oxygen, 6, 13

poison, 44
pollution, 46
puffin, 29; *illus.*, 28

rays, 32
Romans, 22, 44

sand eels, 29; *illus.*, 28
Sargasso Sea, 33, 36, 39, 40;
 illus., 37
seaweed, 36; *illus.*, 37
skeleton, 6, 29
snake eel, 9; *illus.*, 8
snipe eel, 9, 26
spaghetti eels, 10
spawning, 36

tarpon, 6; *illus.*, 7
teeth, 13, 21, 22, 26, 29, 39, 44

vertebrae, 13

Cover: Oxford Scientific Films: Dr. F. Ehrenstrom & L. Beyer.

Photo Credits: Ardea: John Cancalosi 28, Andrea Florence 31; Bruce Coleman: Pacific Stock 16, 20; Corbis: Stephen Frink 11, Roger Wood 45; NHPA: Daniel Heuclin 19, B. Jones & M. Shimlock 15, Trevor McDonald 34/35, Linda & Brian Pitkin 7; Oxford Scientific Films: 12, 37, Paulo De Oliveira 38, David Fleetham 23, Laurence Gould 24, Rodger Jackman 42, C. C. Lockwood/AA 4, Maurice Tibbles/SAL 41; Still Pictures: Jeffrey L. Rotman 27, Norbert Wu 8.